a po

RHYME

Imagination for a new generation

2006 Poetry Competition for 7-11 year-olds

YoungWriters

Northern Rhymes
Edited by Angela Fairbrace

 Young**Writers**

First published in Great Britain in 2007 by:
Young Writers
Remus House
Coltsfoot Drive
Peterborough
PE2 9JX
Telephone: 01733 890066
Website: www.youngwriters.co.uk

All Rights Reserved

© Copyright Contributors 2006

SB ISBN 1 84602 717 9

Foreword

Young Writers was established in 1991 and has been passionately devoted to the promotion of reading and writing in children and young adults ever since. The quest continues today. Young Writers remains as committed to the nurturing of poetic and literary talent as ever.

This year's Young Writers competition has proven as vibrant and dynamic as ever and we are delighted to present a showcase of the best poetry from across the UK and in some cases overseas. Each poem has been selected from a wealth of *A Pocketful Of Rhyme* entries before ultimately being published in this, our fourteenth primary school poetry series.

Once again, we have been supremely impressed by the overall quality of the entries we have received. The imagination, energy and creativity which has gone into each young writer's entry made choosing the poems a challenging and often difficult but ultimately hugely rewarding task - the general high standard of the work submitted ensured this opportunity to bring their poetry to a larger appreciative audience.

We sincerely hope you are pleased with this final collection and that you will enjoy *A Pocketful Of Rhyme Northern Rhymes* for many years to come.

Contents

Omar Mohammed (10)	32
Jonathan Stansfield (9)	32
Zahirah Hafiz (11)	33
Melissa Lowe (10)	33
Ashraf Awgali (10)	33
Oliver Pitts (10)	34
Hanaan Qamar (10)	34
Zaineb Zaffar (10)	35
Reem Mansour (10)	35
Ian Huynh (11)	36
Max Clemmett (10)	36
Leah Mannion (10)	36
Tuseef Ishfaq (10)	37
Sam McDougall (10)	37
Aila Zaib (9)	37
George Mannion (9)	38

Astley St Stephen's CE School, Astley

Isabel Griffin (10)	38
Adam Shepherd (8)	38
Susannah Poole (7)	39
Thomas Gregory (7)	39
Eleanor Callan (8)	40
Luke Getty (8)	40
Mason Shorrock (8)	41
Jack McKerchar (8)	41
Jennifer Ford (7)	41
Hannah Brown (9)	42
Christopher Gore (7)	42
Alice Sharratt (11)	43
Ben Roberts (11)	43
Heather Tyldesley (9)	44
Amy Burgess (9)	44

Belah Primary School, Carlisle

James Brand (10)	45
Louise Ullyart (10)	45
Samantha Wall (10)	46
Becky Chadwick (10)	46
Kathryn Scott-Cowie (10)	47
Thomas Fuller (10)	47

Edward Brand (10)	48
Sophie Kenny (9)	48
Anthony Cropley (10)	49
Jenna Horseman (10)	49
Charlie Prudham (10)	50
Stephen Byers (9)	50
Scott Fawkes (10)	51
Luke Sumpton (10)	51
Lewis Fuller (10)	52
Simon Boothroyd (9)	52
Johanna Armstrong (10)	53
Adam Seymour (8)	53
Camas Millar (9)	54
Joe Ward (9)	54

Markland Hill CP School, Bolton

David Robertson (10)	54
Alex Fisher (10)	55
Daniel Cheetham-Taylor (10)	55
Harriet Dagnall (10)	56
James Boulton (10)	56
Eran Cotterill (10)	57
Jaimie Booth (10)	57
Eleanor Wilson (10)	58
Harry Ward (10)	58
Ben Taylor (10)	59
Bruce Pemberton-Billing (10)	59
Charlie Howe (10)	60
Chloe Smith (10)	60
Drew McGaughey & Rajan Bharaj (10)	61
Hannah Aldcroft (10)	61
Timothy Sinclair (11)	62
Ben Laine (10)	62
Sola Nylander (10)	63
Ellie Schenk (9)	63
Ellie McGivern (9)	63
Java Entwistle (10)	64
Mary Axon-Smith (9)	64
Simon Hind (10)	65
Edward Hayes (10)	65
Anya Cotterill (9)	66

Lucy Entwistle (9)	66
Julia Sabery (9)	66
Leila Safi (9)	67
Robert Swinton (10)	67
Fergus Plant (9)	68
Robert Winteringham (10)	68
Jennifer Walmsley (9)	69
Muhammad Karim (10)	69
Chloe Rothwell (9)	70
Andrew Catterall (10)	70
Callum Rout (9)	71
Niamh Bolton (10)	71
Jack Dawson (9)	72
Jack Hobson (9)	72
Sam Mercer (10)	73

Newton Bluecoat CE Primary School, Newton

Naomi Craven (9)	73
Lauren Sarjantson (10)	73
Samuel Hogarth (9)	74
Russell Townsend (9)	74
Lauren Throup (10)	74
Tawana Gardner (9)	75
Joe Bench (10)	75
Kirsten Milne (9)	75
Rhys Llewellyn (9)	76
Georgia Jameson (10)	76
Brittany Bee (9)	76
James Hayhurst (10)	77
Abbie Ashworth (9)	77
Joe Kearney (10)	77
Matthew Taaffe (10)	78
Catherine Davidson (10)	78
Alex Gamblin Thompson (9)	78
Sophie Thomason (10)	79
Georgia Hallam (9)	79

Oldfield Brow Primary School, Altrincham

Francesca Harrison (10)	79
Robert Shenkman (10)	80

St Mary's RC Primary School, Ulverston

Joshua Bower (10)	80
Peter O'Donovan (10)	81
Nathan Holmes (10)	81
Scott Wilson (9)	81
Abby Stack (11)	82
Jodie Barber (10)	82
Maddy Lackey (9)	83
Bradley Joy (10)	83
Adam Bartlett (9)	84
Carl Postlethwaite (9)	84
Callum Dixon (10)	85
David Wood (9)	85
Charlotte Penellum (10) & Alex Sansom (9)	85
Georgia Moore (9)	86
Megan O'Donovan (9)	86

The Brow CP School, Runcorn

Natalie Reynolds (10)	87
Sophie McGuire (10)	87
Mark Roberts (10)	88
Susannah Pendlebury (10)	88
Sophie Sloan (10)	89
Sam Hall (10)	89
Matthew O'Carroll (10)	90
Jamie Weeder (10)	90
Thomas Grave (10)	91
Ben Crank (11)	91
Courtney Chamberlain (10)	92
Nathan Merdassi (11)	92
Robyn Pattison (10)	93
Joe McNally (10)	93
Shannon Wright (10)	94
Alicia Knox (10)	94

The Poems

Always There

Today is today
Tomorrow will be tomorrow
And yesterday was yesterday
Every day will be the same
Unless . . .
You have those special people . . .
Your family

If you need a favour doing
They'll be there
If you're ill or sad
They'll be there
If you need some help
They will be there

No matter where you are
What you're doing
They will always be there
In the exact place you love them . . .
Your heart.

Emily Nielsen (10)

Umar's Pets

In Umar's bedroom, Umar kept . . .
Ten lions that roared for a long time,
Nine rabbits hopping around the house,
Eight cats chasing the rabbits,
Seven snakes slithering on the chairs,
Six falcons laying eggs,
Five dogs chasing the cats,
Four gorillas jumping on the floor,
Three monkeys making friends with the gorillas,
Two mice running around,
One . . . guess what?

Umar Amjid (8)
Acacias Community Primary School, Burnage

Down Behind The Dustbin

(Based on 'Down Behind the Dustbin' by Michael Rosen)

Down behind the dustbin
I met a dog called Kim.
He stuck his head inside
And came out with a grin.

Down behind the dustbin
I met a dog called Ted.
'Argh!' he cried,
'I want my bed.'

Down behind the dustbin
I met a dog called Daisy.
She was looking
For her cousin Maisy.

Down behind the dustbin
I met a dog called Meg.
She was sitting on the floor
Eating an egg.

Maren Fulton (7)
Acacias Community Primary School, Burnage

Aaron's Pets

In his bedroom, Aaron kept . . .
Ten white mice with cute little pink eyes,
Nine giraffes living in the wardrobe,
Eight squirrels eating nuts in my bed,
Seven hamsters that snoozed in the cage,
Six foxes that are lazy,
Five bats on the light,
Four chickens laying eggs,
Three hedgehogs picking up my socks,
Two caterpillars in my bed,
One puppy in my bed.

Aaron Flowers-Blades (8)
Acacias Community Primary School, Burnage

What Is Orange?

Orange is the colour of
The sweet, sweet tangerines,
They are so healthy
Just like baked beans.

Orange is the colour of
My numeracy books,
With loads of hard sums in them.
This is how they look,
1000,000 x 2,000 ÷ 5 =

Orange is the colour of
A volcano eruption,
With lava spreading everywhere,
There's a big, big commotion.

Muttaqee Dar (8)
Acacias Community Primary School, Burnage

Adam's Pets

In his bedroom Adam kept . . .
Ten caterpillars that ran and hid,
Nine spiders that wore their webs,
Eight white mice with pink tiny eyes,
Seven hamsters that ran around in the cage,
Six brown cats, who were after the rat,
Five small dogs under the bed,
Four pigs, lazy and fat,
Three pythons that hung from the light,
Two donkeys that lived in the wardrobes
And *one* . . . *guess what*?

Adam Wilkinson (8)
Acacias Community Primary School, Burnage

Caitlin's Pets

In Caitlin's bedroom Caitlin kept . . .
Ten frogs that jumped around her bedroom all day long
and all night long,
Nine dogs that barked all night and day,
Eight spiders that were in the bath,
Seven lobsters that crept into the shower,
Six foxes under the bed,
Five ponies at the door,
Four puppies on the carpet,
Three sheep having a barbecue,
Two fish on the wall,
One black cat licking its fur.

Caitlin McAllister (8)
Acacias Community Primary School, Burnage

Harris' Pets

In his bedroom Harris kept . . .
Ten jaguars hiding under the bed,
Nine scorpions in a box,
Eight dogs tearing the pillows,
Seven giraffes trotting around,
Six baboons jumping on the bed,
Five racoons climbing the wall,
Four hedgehogs rolling around,
Three snakes slithering,
Two eagles swooping down
And *one* . . . guess what?

Harris Mohammed (8)
Acacias Community Primary School, Burnage

Nicole's Pets

In her bedroom Nicole kept . . .
Ten elephants which hid in her wardrobe,
Nine donkeys giving children rides,
Eight squirrels eating Nicole's nuts,
Seven koalas hanging on Nicole's roof,
Six snakes on Nicole's wardrobe,
Five hedgehogs on Nicole's shelf,
Four dogs on Nicole's bed,
Three foxes in Nicole's drawers,
Two spiders on Nicole's bed,
One cat on Nicole's wardrobe.

Nicole Barker (8)
Acacias Community Primary School, Burnage

Olivia's Pets

In her bedroom, Olivia kept . . .
Ten glow worms that lit up the room
Nine rabbits that jumped all around
Eight ladybirds that flew all round the room
Seven bulldogs that barked all night
Six squirrels that climbed all over
Five gorillas making a lot of noise
Four giant pigs squeaking all night
Three worms wriggling in my bed
Two owls hooting all night
And *one* . . . guess what?

Olivia Mills (8)
Acacias Community Primary School, Burnage

Mahnoor's Pets

In her bedroom, Mahnoor kept . . .
Ten chinchillas bouncing on the bed,
Nine lobsters who were grabbing my jumper,
Eight chameleons changing colour,
Seven hamsters running on the wheel,
Six pigs pink and fat,
Five smelly cows in my cupboard,
Four cats weeing on my carpet,
Three badgers running everywhere,
Two snakes hung from the light,
One little ant creepy and crawly
And *one* . . . that's me.

Mahnoor Qamar (8)
Acacias Community Primary School, Burnage

Love

Love is pink like sweet fluffy candyfloss
It tastes like a lovely, creamy chocolate bar
It smells like a smooth, tasty peach
It looks like baby chicks tweeting
It reminds me of kindness and Mum and Dad
It sounds like laughter.

Esme Wilson (7)
Acacias Community Primary School, Burnage

Sadness

Sadness is dark blue like the dark sea
It sounds like the waves crashing on the rocks
It tastes like a dead flower
It smells like a person crying
It feels like being lonely
It reminds me of my brother being nasty to me.

Tabitha Hand (7)
Acacias Community Primary School, Burnage

Regan's Poems

In my bedroom I kept . . .
Ten big black bears being grizzly,
Nine slugs sitting on top of my wardrobe slithering,
Eight jaguars lying in my bed - biting,
Seven frogs hopping on my window ledge - jumping a lot,
Six rabbits locked in my wardrobe - running, twitching their nose,
Five zebras jumping on my bed trying to wake the jaguars up,
Four tigers running about - roaring and eating chicken,
Three elephants trying to open the door - bashing and stamping,
Two birds singing on my television - whistling,
One lion running about - spying and roaring.

Regan Lowe (8)
Acacias Community Primary School, Burnage

Happiness

Happiness is yellow like the glazing sun.
Happiness sounds like children having fun.
Happiness tastes like melting chocolate ice cream.
Happiness smells like lavender in the soft breeze.
Happiness looks like berries falling off the berry bush.
Happiness feels like a gentle hand touching me.
Happiness reminds me of my family being cheerful.

Rebecca Phoenix (7)
Acacias Community Primary School, Burnage

Happiness

Happiness is yellow like a bright sun
It tastes like a strawberry
It smells like perfume in a shop
It looks like children playing in the park
It feels like a soft furry teddy
It reminds me of going to a funfair.

Zain Shazad (7)
Acacias Community Primary School, Burnage

What Is Pink?

Pink is a flower
Pink is my tongue
Pink is my lip
Pink is a crayon
Pink is a lunchbox
Pink is my nail
Pink is a pencil case
Pink is a book
Pink is a paint
Pink is a towel
Pink is a lipstick
Pink is a phone
Pink is a bobble
Pink is a rainbow.

Ellis Benjamin (8)
Acacias Community Primary School, Burnage

Blue

Blue is a book
Blue is a jumper
Blue is a pencil crayon
Blue is a milk carton
Blue is a wallpaper
Blue is a door
Blue is the ocean
Blue is the rain
Blue is a pencil case
Blue is a tray
Blue is a carpet
Blue is a car.

Michael Johnstone (8)
Acacias Community Primary School, Burnage

Fun!

I feel like a bouncing ball,
I bounce and bounce,
until I do no more.

My body is jumping about,
if you try and stop me,
I might want to shout.

I'm a funky brown monkey
swinging from tree to tree,
you can't stop me because I'm free!
Would you like to be free like me?

I'm a little race car,
going far and wide,
if you try and stop me,
I might go into overdrive.

Jacob Hand (9)
Acacias Community Primary School, Burnage

Fun!

I feel so alive,
as I jump up and down.
I feel so fit,
I could run like a jaguar.

I pounce, I leap, I jump, I sneak
just like a cheetah does when he hunts!

Just wait and see, you will see me, *pop!*
Like a jack-in-the-box.

The sun shines,
as it dances across the sky,
in its golden yellow ray
and its orange-red glow.

Cairo Lewis (9)
Acacias Community Primary School, Burnage

Sadness

Sadness is grey like a raincloud about to break.
It sounds like the cry of the wind.
It tastes like lemon juice from the finest lemons.
It smells like a dead rabbit with the blood pouring out.
It looks like a woman crying in an enchanted forest.
It feels like your heart breaking apart.
It reminds me of friends breaking up.

Haroon Ahmed (7)
Acacias Community Primary School, Burnage

Hate

Hate is black like the sky, waiting for the sun to come out
Hate sounds like the banging of the drum
Hate tastes like a dinosaur's blood
Hate smells like some rubbish thrown in a smelly bin
Hate looks like a man shouting at his children
Hate feels rough and sharp like a spiky plant
It reminds me of falling out with my friends.

Saima Riaz (7)
Acacias Community Primary School, Burnage

Sadness

Sadness is light blue like the sky in the summer
It sounds like a baby crying in the night
It tastes like a bitter lemon
It smells like a dead flower that's been trodden on
It looks like a tear rolling down my cheek
It feels like a damp wet day
It reminds me of friends breaking up.

Maelyn Warner (7)
Acacias Community Primary School, Burnage

Fear

Fear is green like the long green grass.
Fear sounds like a boy trying to escape from a dark wood.
Fear tastes like a sour apple left in a bin.
Fear smells like some rotten stinky bed.
Fear looks like a black shadow on the wall.
It feels like my knees shivering in winter.
It reminds me of being attacked by a lion.

Nathaniel Smith (7)
Acacias Community Primary School, Burnage

Love

Love is pink like strawberries in the glistening sun
Love sounds like a heart pounding slowly
Love tastes like hot creamy chocolate
Love smells like cold ice cream
Love looks like a soft warm blanket
Love feels warm and cuddly like a pillow
Love reminds me of my mum and dad.

Saman Rizvan (7)
Acacias Community Primary School, Burnage

Fun

Fun is bright yellow like a rainbow shining in the sky.
It sounds like children laughing a lot.
It tastes like creamy chocolate about to go down my throat.
It smells like jelly ice cream that I want to smell.
It looks like happy people eating jelly sweets.
It feels fun to bounce on a bouncy castle and have a party.
It reminds me of all the happy times with my family and friends.

Zainab Ahmed (7)
Acacias Community Primary School, Burnage

Anger

Anger is red like a blazing red fire.
It sounds like thunder shouting in your ears.
It tastes like sour sweets in your mouth.
It smells like burnt toast near your nose.
It looks like lightning in front of your eyes.
It feels like a large rock in your hands.
It reminds me of thunder in the air.

Zain Amin (7)
Acacias Community Primary School, Burnage

Darkness

Darkness is black like a wintry, scary bat.
Darkness sounds like a ghost in the dark.
Darkness tastes like a rotten apple.
Darkness smells like rats in their hole.
Darkness looks like pitch-black night.
Darkness feels like a furry spider in the dark.
Darkness reminds me of being alone with no light.

Maarya Amyid (7)
Acacias Community Primary School, Burnage

Hate

Hate is black like a dead rat in the dark.
It sounds like a knife cutting a loaf of bread.
It tastes like a sharp throat and it's hurting my fingers.
It smells like someone's smelly feet.
It looks like disgusting dead fish.
It feels like a rhino chasing me.
It reminds me of my sister chasing me.

Umar Hafiz (7)
Acacias Community Primary School, Burnage

Darkness

Darkness is black like a night with dusk on it.
Darkness is like mud with dust in it.
What does it sound like? Dark all over the place.
What does it taste like? It tastes like mud, very dark mud.
What does it smell like? It smells like smelly old mud.
What does it look like? It looks like mud, squelchy mud.
What does it feel like? It feels like sticky mud.
What does it remind you of? It reminds me of darkness.

Shaffan Iqbal (7)
Acacias Community Primary School, Burnage

Fear

Fear is dark blue like the deep, dark, silver ocean
It sounds like a bat with fierce wings
It tastes like a bitter, juicy lemon running down my throat
It smells like a dirty plum tree
It looks like a dark, scary, howling night
It feels like rough, hard cardboard
It reminds me of a big, disgusting worm.

Jessica Hand (7)
Acacias Community Primary School, Burnage

Fear

Fear is green like seaweed sliming on your feet
It sounds like owls howling away to the moon.
It tastes like my tongue's really dried up.
It smells like danger blowing in my ears.
It looks like my heart's pounding cautiously.
It feels like a shivering earthquake.
It reminds me of hairy insects crawling on me.

Nabila Jahan Juhi (7)
Acacias Community Primary School, Burnage

Fear

Fear is black like the dark winter sky,
It sounds like stamping in a dungeon.
It tastes like bitter lime,
It smells like dried blood.
It looks like a tall skyscraper,
It feels like shivery knees,
It reminds me of being attacked.

Matthew Clarke (7)
Acacias Community Primary School, Burnage

Fun

Fun is happy like a birthday party,
It sounds like a balloon popping.
It tastes of delicious food cooking.
It smells like air that's in a bouncy castle,
It looks exciting.
It feels like happiness,
It reminds me of playing football with my friends.

Junaid Hafiz (7)
Acacias Community Primary School, Burnage

Love

Love is red like a heart
Beating loudly like a drum.
A taste of chocolate
With a smell of ice cream.
Love looks like red roses
And feels soft and warm.
Love reminds me of my family.

Jihan Ahmed (7)
Acacias Community Primary School, Burnage

Fun

I feel happy like a monkey
Swinging from tree to tree
And nobody can stop me.
Fun, fun, fun as can be
I'm having fun, whoopee!

It's sunny outside,
Let's go to play on my bike,
Riding up and down the hill.

I feel like I can fly to Brazil,
I can fly high, high,
In the clear sky.
Why, why do I think I can fly?
I don't know,
But I'm sure I can.

My body feels like it's full of energy
And I need to release it somehow.
I know, I'll go jogging!

Omar Akram (9)
Acacias Community Primary School, Burnage

Fun

My body is filled with energy, so many things to do,
Lots and lots of options of things to do.
I'm rushing around like a fast cheetah
Having so much fun.
I feel like a monkey swinging from branches
With a gargantuan smile on my face.
I feel like a ray of sunshine shining on the beach.
I feel like a bubble floating in the air
But never popping.

Kiera Bell (9)
Acacias Community Primary School, Burnage

Fun!

Fun is a smiley face,
Fun is a jumpy feeling inside,
Fun is giddiness in your head,
Fun is an exciting thing.

Monkeys know how to have fun,
Monkeys swing from trees making funny noises,
Monkeys show their pink bottoms and don't care,
Monkeys are the most fun-filled animals I can think of.

When I have fun I feel like a clown at the circus,
When I have fun I feel like a firework exploding,
When I have fun I feel like shouting, 'Yeah!'
When I have fun I feel beautiful.

Fun is galloping like a horse,
Fun is swinging on a swing,
Therefore,
Fun is everywhere!
Don't you think?

Jake Connell (9)
Acacias Community Primary School, Burnage

The Witches' Spell

(Inspired by Macbeth)

'Double, double, toil and trouble,
Fire burn and cauldron bubble'.
Measles spots off a human
And a brain of an ostrich,
Blood of a rhino and bum of a fish,
Guts of a wolf and teeth of Dracula,
A tongue of a lion and fur of a dog,
Beak of a duck and feathers of an eagle,
Spikes of a hedgehog and skin of a tiger,
Head of Lucy and a beak of a chicken.

Anthony Harrod-Callam (8)
Acacias Community Primary School, Burnage

The Witches' Spell

'Double, double, toil and trouble'.
Take a pinch of alligator's teeth and stir in the cauldron,
Chop up the elephant feet and throw into the brew,
Melt dogs' heads and throw it into the potion,
Pour the blood of cow into the cauldron,
Add more wood to the fire and simmer for six months.
When it is ready use the potion to destroy the universe
And become king!
'Double double toil and trouble,
Fire burn and cauldron bubble'.

Jibril Ahmed (8)
Acacias Community Primary School, Burnage

Sadness

Sadness is black like a creepy spider
Squeaking across the living room floor.
It tastes like onions and smells like dying flowers.
Sadness looks like somebody crying
And feels like somebody is sad.
Sadness reminds me of when my baby died.

Remi Walton (7)
Acacias Community Primary School, Burnage

Love

Love is pink like shiny crystals in the bright sun
It sounds like a charming tune in the gentle breeze
It smells like daisies in the nice fresh air
It looks like my gills are floating away like some waves
It feels like a warm hot-water bottle that I snuggle in with at night
It reminds me of my family.

Anam Akhtar (7)
Acacias Community Primary School, Burnage

The Witches' Spell

(Inspired by Macbeth)

'Double, double, toil and trouble,
Fire burn and cauldron bubble.'
Werewolves' howls and pixies' brains,
Devil's towel and mane of lion,
Making my day with witch's broom
And then go into vampire's tomb.
A fiery heart and a gremlin's head,
Then add a dragon's bed,
Rinse it all with a pig's ring too
And then a neck of a horse
And a scorpion's sting
With a hair, only blond,
And then with a wizard's wand.
Then mix the most evil skull of Hell,
Then kill a gremlin and steal its bell,
Then kill a lion and steal its skull,
Then add a mean black cat,
Then a fruit bat,
'Double, double, toil and trouble,
Fire burn and cauldron bubble.'

Derand Demaj (9)
Acacias Community Primary School, Burnage

The Witches' Spell

(Inspired by Macbeth)

'Double, double, toil and trouble,
fire burn and cauldron bubble.'
Feet of werewolves and skin of crocodile,
heart of dinosaur and brain of ape,
eye of wolf and teeth of vampires,
tail of reptile and feet of Bigfoot,
wings of dragon and frogspawn,
face of slimy toad and arms of gorilla,
chest of burning and knife of killing.

Mohammed Awais Ahmed (9)
Acacias Community Primary School, Burnage

The Witches' Spell

(Inspired by Macbeth)

'Double, double, toil and trouble,
Fire burn and cauldron bubble'.
Stomach of a cow, octopus' legs,
Eyes of jellyfish, dog eggs,
Feet of a zombie, frozen flies,
Vampire teeth and elephant eyes,
Teeth of a shark, dog bed,
Gypsy feet, rat's head,
Dragon spine, ostrich brain,
Giraffe's tongue, lion's mane,
Rhino's horn, shark's gut,
Cat's whiskers, tiger's butt,
'Like a hell-broth, boil and bubble.
Double, double, toil and trouble,
Fire burn and cauldron bubble'.

Sabrina Chowdhury (9)
Acacias Community Primary School, Burnage

The Witches' Spell

(Inspired by Macbeth)

'Double, double, toil and trouble,
Fire burn and cauldron bubble'.
Legs from a frog and a wormy boot,
A foot from an elephant and a dirty hoot,
Vein from a dog and a mane from a lion,
Teeth from a wolf and a brain from a whale,
An eye from a shark and a pot of goo,
Ear from a human and some sloppy poo.
'Double, double, toil and trouble,
Fire burn and cauldron bubble'.

Rachel Massey (8)
Acacias Community Primary School, Burnage

The Witches' Spell

(Inspired by Macbeth)

'Double, double, toil and trouble,
Fire burn and cauldron bubble'.
Snail's eye and dog tongue pie,
A full moon and a big cocoon,
Teeth of a dog and a big brown leaf,
A wormy boot and a horse's tail,
And a stormy gale.
A McVitie's biscuit and some Alaskan snow,
A human bone and an ice cream cone,
A star from the sky, a human must die,
A thief's money and Richard Dunny,
Basil Brush's tail and a big green whale.
'Double, double, toil and trouble,
Fire burn and cauldron bubble'.

Anna Wijnhoven (9)
Acacias Community Primary School, Burnage

The Witches' Spell

(Inspired by Macbeth)

'Double, double, toil and trouble,
Fire burn and cauldron bubble'.
Tail of a newt, paws of a lion,
Eyeballs of Anthony and whiskers of a cat,
Guts of Superman and brain of an alien,
Hooves of a giraffe, beak of a falcon,
Teeth of a tiger, body of Malcolm,
The arms of John and a crow's wing,
Head of Lucy and scorpion's sting,
'Double, double, toil and trouble,
Fire burn and cauldron bubble'.

Toby Adesunloye (8)
Acacias Community Primary School, Burnage

The Witches' Spell

(Inspired by Macbeth)

'Double, double, toil and trouble,
Fire burn and cauldron bubble'.
Heart of goat and lungs of alligator,
Fin of a shark and hump of camel.
Head of Mr Stanley and liver from a baby,
Wing of ostrich and cry of baby,
Teeth of vampire and eyes of lady,
Heart of monkey and blood from a monkey,
Heart from a baby and nose of dwarf,
Heart of dwarf and liver of goat.
'Double, double, toil and trouble,
Fire burn and cauldron bubble'.

Rhea Walton (8)
Acacias Community Primary School, Burnage

The Witches' Spell

(Inspired by Macbeth)

'Double, double, toil and trouble,
Fire burn and cauldron bubble'.
Eye of chicken, brain of a monkey,
Lion's mane, alligator's teeth,
Wing of a bat, baby's hair,
Chocolate spread with melted bread,
A gorilla's heart that's very sharp,
Snake's brain with a slice of pain,
King's hairy legs, ewww, look at them,
Elephant's ears, what long things.
'Double, double, toil and trouble,
Fire burn and cauldron bubble'.

Simran Singh (8)
Acacias Community Primary School, Burnage

The Witches' Spell

(Inspired by Macbeth)

'Double, double, toil and trouble,
Fire burn and cauldron bubble.'
Tongue of a goblin and put in some frogs,
Mane of a lion, mix around,
Make this potion to destroy the world.
'Double, double, toil and trouble,
Fire burn and cauldron bubble.'

Daniel Dunn (8)
Acacias Community Primary School, Burnage

Rainbow

Rainbow,
Leads to a pot of gold,
Colourful, magical, sparkly,
Like stripes of paint towering above us,
Like swathes of colourful fabric flying,
It makes me feel warm inside,
Reminds me of the beauty of colour.

Bethany Williams (10)
Acacias Community Primary School, Burnage

The Witches' Spell

(Inspired by Macbeth)

'Double, double, toil and trouble,
Fire burn and cauldron bubble.'
A toe of a frog, a horn of a rhino,
Fin of a shrimp and blood from a cow,
A neck of a giraffe, ears from an elephant.
'Double, double, toil and trouble,
Fire burn and cauldron bubble.'

Is'haaq Khan (8)
Acacias Community Primary School, Burnage

The Universe

The universe
No start and no finish
Spacious, colossal, phenomenal
As huge as infinity
Like an everlasting world
I feel diminutive
Like a speck of dust
The universe
Reminds us of God's amazing creations.

Rui Ding (11)
Acacias Community Primary School, Burnage

Fun

Fun is yellow like the hot shining sun,
It sounds like a funfair with giant rides,
The taste is like the sweetest candyfloss,
It reminds me of playing football with my friends,
It feels like having two birthdays,
In my mind it looks like an enormous swimming pool,
The smell is like hot chocolate cake.

Hamzah Khanzada (9)
Acacias Community Primary School, Burnage

Fear

The colour of fear is dark red.
The sound of fear is hot orange lava.
The taste of fear is fizzy Coke.
The smell of fear is choking smoke.
The fear looks like hot, burning fire.
The fear feels like the fearing dark.
The fear reminds me of the fearing anger.

Mufaddal Yamani (9)
Acacias Community Primary School, Burnage

The Witches' Spell

(Inspired by Macbeth)

'Double, double, toil and trouble,
Fire burn and cauldron bubble.'
Eye of dolphin and shoe of horse,
Feather of peacock and brain of cat,
Tongue of dog and lung of ostrich,
Tail of donkey and mane of lion,
Ear of devil and arm of human,
Head of camel and neck of giraffe,
Slime of slug and shell of snail,
Blood of human and teeth of dog,
Body of a monster and heart of elephant,
Soul of toad and bones of skeleton.
'Double, double, toil and trouble,
Fire burn and cauldron bubble.'

Sofia Ahmed (9)
Acacias Community Primary School, Burnage

Mount Fugi

Mount Fugi
Stood for many years
Huge, mighty, magnificent
Like a plane flying in the clouds
Like God's thumb from Heaven
It makes me feel small
Like an ant about to be stood on
Mount Fugi
Reminds us how small we are.

Robert Birkett (10)
Acacias Community Primary School, Burnage

The Witches' Spell
(Inspired by Macbeth)

'Double, double, toil and trouble,
Fire burn and cauldron bubble.'
A hippo tooth and Pegasus' hoof,
Seven pigs' ears and a horse's tail,
Lions' whiskers and a big blue whale.
Now mix in some Dalmatian spots,
A dragon's head and a drop of cat's blood,
A lizard's foot and a plank of wood.
Now a pinch of salt and the Devil's brain to give out a fiery flame.
Oh what a surprise, who could forget
Dragon eyes, toad guts and a monster's butt.
A pretty pink dress and a bottle of water,
A big red apple and a lamb to the slaughter.
'Double, double, toil and trouble,
Fire burn and cauldron bubble.'

Megan Booth (8)
Acacias Community Primary School, Burnage

The Witches' Spell
(Inspired by Macbeth)

Double, double, hop in my bubble,
Fire burn of a fenny snake like a
Hell broth and a blind worm's sting,
A man's big brain and a frog's leg,
A bird's neck, vampire's teeth,
A famous king's crown, baby guts,
A fat human's head and a shark's jaw,
'Double, double, toil and trouble,
Fire burn and cauldron bubble.'

Daniel Bryan (8)
Acacias Community Primary School, Burnage

The Witches' Spell

(Inspired by Macbeth)

'Double, double, toil and trouble,
Fire burn and cauldron bubble.'
Shell of a snail and human snot,
Gills of a fish and leopards' spots,
Wool of a sheep and dragon spikes,
Slime from a slug and animals' likes,
Wings from a bat and croc's teeth,
Manure from a cow and a mint leaf,
Ears from a baby and a metal mouth,
A book of maths and a boy called Alf,
A leotard from a dancer and a robot of metal.
'Double, double, toil and trouble,
Fire burn and cauldron bubble.'

Lucy Ridding (8)
Acacias Community Primary School, Burnage

The Witches' Spell

(Inspired by Macbeth)

'Double, double, toil and trouble,
Fire burn and cauldron bubble.'
Horn of a rhino and pigs' trotters,
Blood of an ostrich and baby otters,
Tail of a devil and frogs' brains,
Slime of a snail and human veins,
Legs of an octopus and giraffe skin,
Ear of an elephant and human grins.
'Double, double, toil and trouble,
Fire burn and cauldron bubble.'

Ruby Sacofsky (8)
Acacias Community Primary School, Burnage

Shooting Stars

Shooting stars
Only come out at night
Radiant, minute, enjoyable
Like an arrow shooting through the sky
As rapid as a cheetah
It makes my day go bright
As bright as the sun
Shooting stars
Remind me of fireworks.

Sara Ejaz (10)
Acacias Community Primary School, Burnage

Love

Love is red and pink like a flower,
Love smells like chocolate in my hands,
Love looks like melting chocolate in the room,
Love reminds me of a beautiful holiday,
Love feels really comfortable,
Love tastes like really cold ice cream,
Love sounds like love music.

Charlotte Stennings (10)
Acacias Community Primary School, Burnage

Darkness

Darkness is pitch-black like a shadow leaning over you.
Darkness sounds like footsteps which are coming closer.
Darkness tastes sickening like a drop of poison.
Darkness smells like a fire burning ever so quickly.
Darkness looks empty like being alone in a dark room.
Darkness feels like fear that is threatening you every second.
Darkness reminds me of ghosts haunting you all the time.

Briony Byrne (10)
Acacias Community Primary School, Burnage

Mount Everest

Mount Everest . . .
The biggest mountain in the world,
Mountainous, gargantuan, immeasurable,
Like a skyscraper reaching the sky,
Like an arrow pointing to Heaven,
It makes me feel like a micro-organism,
Like a speck of dust.
Mount Everest
Reminds us of how polite we are.

Sonia Rahman (10)
Acacias Community Primary School, Burnage

What Is Love?

Love is red and pink like fire burning and sweet candyfloss,
It sounds like birds tweeting on a Sunday morning.
Love tastes like chocolate melting in my mouth,
It smells like roses blowing in the breeze.
Love looks like children playing happily in the playground,
It feels like fur coats brushing against my face.
Love reminds me of angels singing in the heavens,
That is what I think of love!

Courtney Tetlow (9)
Acacias Community Primary School, Burnage

Darkness

Darkness is black like a shadow.
Darkness sounds threatening like a bully.
Darkness tastes poisoning with a dying effect.
Darkness smells blank like an empty room.
Darkness looks empty like you're scariest.
Darkness feels lonely like you're on your own.
Darkness reminds me of nothing, like nothing is there.

Abbie Wheelton (10)
Acacias Community Primary School, Burnage

Darkness

Darkness is black like a darkening volcano.
Darkness is the clashing of swords in a terrible battle.
Darkness is the taste of burnt orange lava.
Darkness is the smell of fiery rising dust.
Darkness is fire, blazing-hot, red and black.
Darkness is like going back in time,
Seeing the world from the past.
Darkness is the dusk of midnight,
Pitch-black, no light.

Vincent Curran-French (9)
Acacias Community Primary School, Burnage

The Exquisite Cat

The exquisite cat
Was an Egyptian god,
Adorable, pleasing, fleecy,
As soft as silk,
As precious as a diamond,
It makes me feel happy,
That it seeks me for safety,
The exquisite cat,
Reminds me of God's creations.

Aisha Qazzafi (10)
Acacias Community Primary School, Burnage

Anger

The colour of anger is red like a devil's face
And it sounds like a dragon roaring.
It tastes of sweat and blood mixed up together,
It also smells of breaking, rotten bones which are hard and brown,
It feels rough like a huge cat's teeth
And it reminds me of my sister annoying me.

Humza Jauhar (9)
Acacias Community Primary School, Burnage

The Sky

The sky
It has always been there,
Expansive, cloudy, exquisite,
It's like a sea in the sky,
As blue as a sapphire,
It makes me feel microscopic,
As small as the Earth to the sun,
The sky,
Reminds us how we got atmosphere.

Cameron James Lennox (10)
Acacias Community Primary School, Burnage

Big Ben

Big Ben
Tallest clock in England,
Enormous, mighty, majestic,
As tall as a tower,
Like an arrow pointing to space,
It makes me feel microscopic,
It makes me feel like a dot on a page,
Big Ben
Reminds me of time.

Jack Cookson (10)
Acacias Community Primary School, Burnage

Darkness

Darkness is black like a vampire's cape,
It sounds like the Devil's laughter waiting to kill.
It tastes of lava spitting to the ground,
It looks like blood lying still.
It reminds me of the underworld, infested with monsters,
It feels like breath crawling up my back,
It smells like gunshots being shot at soldiers.

Matthew Orme (10)
Acacias Community Primary School, Burnage

The Beach

The beach,
Sand near the sea,
Glorious, soft, flaxen,
As gold as the sun,
As soft as the snow,
It makes me feel delighted,
Like children making sandcastles.
The beach,
Please keep it safe from litter.

Tanzeela Khan (10)
Acacias Community Primary School, Burnage

Happiness

Happiness is yellow like the beaming of the sun,
It sounds like jumping with excitement, like shouting with drums.
Happiness tastes of sweets like the lovely honey food,
It smells of roses like the fresh beautiful flowers.
Happiness looks like stars that are bright and yellow,
It feels like sand, like the soft smooth texture.
Happiness reminds me of children playing,
Exciting and enjoying.

Giny Huynh (9)
Acacias Community Primary School, Burnage

Big Ben

London's largest clock,
Gargantuan, powerful, on top of the world
Like an expansive tower,
Like a knife shooting at the sky.
It makes me feel tiny
Like a grain of salt.
Big Ben
Reminds us how important time is.

Trey Shelton (10)
Acacias Community Primary School, Burnage

The Earth

The Earth
It is a spherical shaped planet,
Huge, mighty, powerful,
Like a ball in space,
Floating like a cloud,
It makes me feel microscopic
Like a grain of dust.
The Earth,
Reminds us how final our lives are.

Liam Morgan (10)
Acacias Community Primary School, Burnage

The River Nile

The River Nile,
The world's longest river,
Expansive, interminable, old
Like a spiralling serpent,
Like a winding road,
It makes me feel small
Like a tiny ant.
The River Nile,
It reminds us how amazing rivers are.

Omar Mohammed (10)
Acacias Community Primary School, Burnage

Anger

Anger is red like a hot burning fire on a November day,
It sounds like a firework on Guy Fawkes night
And tastes like ashes on a cigarette just been finished.
It smells like a boiling fire on a winter's night,
It looks like a volcano just exploded,
It feels like chucking something,
It reminds me of an exploding volcano.

Jonathan Stansfield (9)
Acacias Community Primary School, Burnage

The Mighty Tiger

The mighty tiger,
A huge, wild cat,
Guileful, vigorous, proud
Like a king striding through the town,
Like a warrior ready to rip you to shreds,
It makes me feel anxious
Like a fly in front of a spider waiting to be devoured.
The mighty tiger
Reminds me how amazing wildlife is.

Zahirah Hafiz (11)
Acacias Community Primary School, Burnage

The Sea

The sea,
The sea covers two thirds of the world,
Dark, deep, dangerous
Like a blue blanket covering the Earth,
Like a desert of water.
It makes me feel tiny
Like a drip of water.
The sea
Reminds me to wonder at God's creation.

Melissa Lowe (10)
Acacias Community Primary School, Burnage

Silence

Silence is like an ocean waving on you,
Silence looks like a bright white cloud shining,
Silence smells like cold,
Silence tastes like water,
Silence sounds like rain rushing down on you,
Silence feels calm,
Silence reminds me of people who died in war.

Ashraf Awgali (10)
Acacias Community Primary School, Burnage

The Sun

The sun,
Over one thousand degrees,
Boiling, blazing, burning
Like a majestic ball of flames.
As hot as a volcano,
It makes me feel warm
Like a cat in front of a fire.
The sun,
It reminds me how huge space is.

Oliver Pitts (10)
Acacias Community Primary School, Burnage

The Sun

The sun,
The hottest star,
Scorching, vast, majestic,
As hot as a volcano,
Like a fireball floating in space.
It makes me feel like a lump of dust,
As microscopic as a grain of sand.
The sun
Reminds me what gives the world light.

Hanaan Qamar (10)
Acacias Community Primary School, Burnage

The Sea

The sea,
It surrounds us,
Blue, deep, enormous
Like a large blue blanket.
As glittery as jewels,
It makes me feel amazed
With awe and wonder.
The sea
It reminds me of
The mystery of creation.

Zaineb Zaffar (10)
Acacias Community Primary School, Burnage

Mount Everest

Mount Everest
The tallest mountain in the world,
Elevated, immense, powerful
Like an arrow shooting at space,
Like a tower pointing at the sky.
It makes me feel petite
Like a speck of dust.
Mount Everest
Reminds us how vast the Earth can be.

Reem Mansour (10)
Acacias Community Primary School, Burnage

The Equator

The Equator,
The hottest place on Earth,
Boiling, scorching, deserted
Like an oven,
Like a line of gunpowder.
It makes me feel wonder,
Amazed at its length.
The Equator
Reminds us there are no limits to the Earth.

Ian Huynh (11)
Acacias Community Primary School, Burnage

Elephant

The enormous elephant
Has lived for ages,
Enormous, heavy, strong
Like a tank in the wild,
Like a moving wall.
It makes me feel weak
Like a baby that can't fight.
The enormous elephant
Reminds us how weak we are.

Max Clemmett (10)
Acacias Community Primary School, Burnage

The Ocean

Full of beautiful fish
Deep, dark, dangerous
As cold as an ice cube
Like a blanket covering the Earth
I wonder at the mystery of its depth
The ocean
It reminds me how minute we are compared to the ocean.

Leah Mannion (10)
Acacias Community Primary School, Burnage

Cheetah

Cheetah,
The fastest animal
Full tilt, rapid, swift,
As brisk as a bullet,
Like a shooting star.
I feel frightened of its power
Predatory instinct.
Cheetah,
Save it from extinction.

Tuseef Ishfaq (10)
Acacias Community Primary School, Burnage

The Sun

The sun,
The hottest star,
Gigantic, blazing, roasting
Like an enormous ball of gas,
Like a giant bonfire.
I feel joyful when the sun is out
Like a lizard lying in the sun.
The sun
Reminds us how we get light and warmth.

Sam McDougall (10)
Acacias Community Primary School, Burnage

Happiness

Happiness is light blue,
Happiness is peace,
Happiness sounds like laughter and is joyful,
Happiness tastes like I'm delighted,
Happiness smells like beautiful flowers,
Happiness looks like a sun shining brightly in the clear sky,
Happiness reminds me of holidays.

Aila Zaib (9)
Acacias Community Primary School, Burnage

The Witches' Spell
(Inspired by Macbeth)

'Double, double, toil and trouble,
Fire burn and cauldron bubble'.
Bones of a dinosaur and legs of a lizard,
Blood of a chicken and webbed feet,
Lots of meat to eat,
Spikes of a conker shell and a screaming shout,
Frogspawn growing all about.

George Mannion (9)
Acacias Community Primary School, Burnage

Floating Feather

The floating feather
Soft, silent, stolen
Like a gentle wave breaking on the shore
Like a pale bird drifting in the sky
Safe and strong
Like silk spun in a spider's web
A single soft touch of a dove
The floating feather
A gift from Heaven.

Isabel Griffin (10)
Astley St Stephen's CE School, Astley

Fireworks

Fizzing like a shaken-up can of pop
Jumping like a mad kangaroo
Swooping like a golden eagle high in the sky
Swirling like a huge whirlpool
Screaming like a terrified ghost
Zipping like speeding cars
Dying in a cloud of smoke.

Adam Shepherd (8)
Astley St Stephen's CE School, Astley

The Ancient Castle

Suits of armour rattle and shake,
A rattlesnake hisses and splutters,
Cobwebs spun by giant spiders
Hang from the corners of every room,
Curiosity, people say,
Can mean death,
Ghosts fly through cold air
In silent corridors,
Bones crumble in old cellars,
So take my advice
There is danger
Beware.

Susannah Poole (7)
Astley St Stephen's CE School, Astley

Night-Time Is . . .

A ghost walking a deserted street
A silent mist creeping by
A bat that swoops and dives
Clouds floating like grey feathers
Stars like thrown away, gold sweet wrappers
An owl's hoot in the empty dark
A silver moon like polished coin
A river twisting and twinkling
Evil red eyes that watch
A poisonous spider spinning a web
A mysterious dragon that hides in the dark.

Thomas Gregory (7)
Astley St Stephen's CE School, Astley

Cellar

Peer into the cellar
Of the haunted house
Creep down steps
That are grim and dark
Grasping hands pull you in
Doors creak
By themselves
Down below
Long, slimy pythons wait
Curled on old, rotting chairs
A mouldy old wine bottle
Drips in the dark
And a silent game of chess
Plays on a worn-out table
Moved by ghostly hands
In the dark cellar.

Eleanor Callan (8)
Astley St Stephen's CE School, Astley

The Woods

Beware
In the spooky woods there are branches that creep
Through fallen piles of old, dead leaves
They reach out to grab your knees
There are cobwebs hanging from tree to tree
Sticky traps made for me
There are silent mists that float like feathers
And bats that will swoop like an aeroplane
Deep in the woods red eyes stare
So beware
Of the darkness that lies there
Enter if you dare.

Luke Getty (8)
Astley St Stephen's CE School, Astley

Night

Stars glitter
Exploding like a rainbow of fireworks
Following a setting sun
As the moon arrives
And all is silent in the town
If you listen closely
A swooping owl hoots
A hungry fox howls
A lonely frog croaks
Tonight.

Mason Shorrock (8)
Astley St Stephen's CE School, Astley

Night River

Stars glitter like diamonds on rings
Clouds float like fluffy candyfloss
Owls hoot like the horn of a speeding train
Bats swoop like target missiles
Mist creeps like a ghostly hand
The moon shines like a single headlight
As down below the river twists and turns
Like a boa constrictor.

Jack McKerchar (8)
Astley St Stephen's CE School, Astley

Starlight

Glistening gems on precious rings
Twinkling lights that shine out bright
Gleaming, glowing
Dancing like twirling ballerinas
Swooping like bats' eyes very bright
In a moonless night sky.

Jennifer Ford (7)
Astley St Stephen's CE School, Astley

Shopping

Doors open wide
People flow in
Gushing and rushing
To reach destinations
Toy shops flood
With pocket-money grasping children
Clothes shops bubble
With fashion victims
While others meander
Taking their time
A gentle ripple of noise
End of the day
People gradually float and drift away
All is still
Calm
Silent.

Hannah Brown (9)
Astley St Stephen's CE School, Astley

Bats

Creatures of the night
Private jet planes
Swooping and gliding
Eyes that glow like a torch
Hidden like a chameleon in the branch of a tree
Hanging
Waiting
A diving rocket
A racing car
A swirling spinning top
Snatching an insect
Eating like a tree-chopping chainsaw.

Christopher Gore (7)
Astley St Stephen's CE School, Astley

The Decorative Butterfly

Transforming
From a tiny caterpillar
Delicate
Fragile
Precious
The floating of a feather
Through a whispering breeze
Wings the work
Of an unseen painter
Light as the air
That tickles my hand
A spring day
Of new life.

Alice Sharratt (11)
Astley St Stephen's CE School, Astley

The Match

Floodlights flare
A warning
As the opposing fans burn with anger.
The ball rumbles into the net,
The Kop explodes!
Excitement!
The manager erupts onto the sidelines.
The match ends.
The opposing fans melt with disappointment
As we glow with happiness.
Liverpool 3 United 0.

Ben Roberts (11)
Astley St Stephen's CE School, Astley

The Last Daisy Of Summer

The last daisy's
Snow-white petals
Attract miniaturised creatures
Faded, frightened, fragile

Like the touch of a crumbling leaf
On a child's cheek
Like a tiny spider shedding
Its abandoned skin.

Makes me feel powerful
Like the Empire State Building
As the lights flare.

The last daisy of summer
Reminds me how delicate life is.

Heather Tyldesley (9)
Astley St Stephen's CE School, Astley

The Beautiful Butterfly

The beautiful butterfly
Lays its fragile eggs on a dawn-fresh leaf
Delicate, silky, rainbow
Golden wings like colourful ribbons drifting in a breeze
Two furry antennae wiggle
As tissue wings open on new day sun
Making me feel warm inside
Dainty as diamond dewdrops
On a spider-spun web
The beautiful butterfly
Reminds me of spring's burst
Of rich, bold flowers.

Amy Burgess (9)
Astley St Stephen's CE School, Astley

Monkeys

Monkeys in the canopy
Swinging tree to tree
Short tails, long tails,
Wrap round the tree.

Monkeys in the treetops
Moving tree to tree
While searching for food
In the jungle as they are free.

Monkeys on the ground moving so swiftly
As they head to the water hole
For a drink and a morning stroll
At the water hole.

A man in the bushes with a knife
And the monkeys shout, 'Run for your life.'
As the man moves closer
The monkey glance at the knife in terror
Run for your life!

James Brand (10)
Belah Primary School, Carlisle

Holidays

Holidays are such good fun, lots of
Fun for everyone, I love the sun
I love the sea, holidays are
Great for me! Ice cream
Lollipops and all
Kinds of things,
Lovely for
A treat,
So if
You
Would like
A treat go on a . . .
Holiday!

Louise Ullyart (10)
Belah Primary School, Carlisle

Dreams

Some dreams I like,
Some dreams I hate,
Especially when I dream of,
My mother's cooking on my plate.

Some people dream of being famous,
Lizzy McGuire, Girls Aloud they wish,
I just dream of being outrageous,
Like wearing all different kinds of nail varnish.

Some people have dreams, really bad dreams,
Like meeting a monster in a dark, gloomy wood.
You want to wake up,
And when you do you suddenly sit right up.

I love to hear people's dreams,
Good, exciting, scary and bad.
But I don't like the ones,
That make you feel sad.

People dream every night,
Especially when,
I'm cuddled up tight,
That's why people dream.

Samantha Wall (10)
Belah Primary School, Carlisle

Dolphins

D olphins are great at swimming
O ver the waves they go
L ove skimming
P ast the others they flow.
H ear them squeak,
I n the ocean there's
N othing better than playing hide-and-seek,
S wimming in pairs.

Becky Chadwick (10)
Belah Primary School, Carlisle

Roller Coaster

R ight at the front, the waiting is nearly over
O range, green, pink and purple rushing past my eyes
L ong queues behind me, reaching all the way to Dover.
L emon-coloured cart next but I want the red one,
   I want the red one.
E xcited I get in my seat longing to go all by myself
R eady . . . and *whoosh* we've gone.

C huga-chuga up the high hill round the corner and *whoosh*
                                       back down,
O range cart behind us, but I know it won't crash and bash
A t the curve and my nervousness is coming round
S creaming I go round and round
T errified I think *when will it end*?
E xhausted and it's nearly the end
R eady and rest.

Kathryn Scott-Cowie (10)
Belah Primary School, Carlisle

A Forest Of Wood

A ll of the forest is cold and dark,

F loor of the forest is covered with old bark.
O ld trees sway and move,
R otten conkers hit horse's hooves.
E xtremely tall trees,
S mall buzzing bees.
T he forest is a scary place.

O ak trees get chopped down,
F or the queen to hold her crown.

W ood is used for lots of things,
O live trees are small but not as small as rings.
O ak trees are mainly in England,
D o you know the forest as well as the back of your hand?

Thomas Fuller (10)
Belah Primary School, Carlisle

Birds

Birds in the bird bath
What a splash they make.
Tail feathers, wing feathers
Shake, shake, shake.

Birds at the feeder
Steady on their feet.
Red birds, yellow birds,
Eat, eat, eat.

Birds in the treetops.
On the beach, in the sky.
Birds run, birds wade, birds
Fly, fly, fly.

Birds that live in water.
Birds that search and dig.
Ostriches and eagles
Big, big, big.

Birds that chirp and warble.
Birds that tweet and sing.
Birds that talk by flapping
A wing, wing, wing.

Edward Brand (10)
Belah Primary School, Carlisle

Dolphin

D own in the sea
O ctopi and dolphins
L aughing and
P laying
H unting for seaweed
I n the bushes
N ever getting caught in nets.

Sophie Kenny (9)
Belah Primary School, Carlisle

Numeracy Poem

Numeracy is fun,
Under the bright yellow sun.
Numeracy is great,
And has an outstanding rate.

Numeracy makes you smart,
You get a powerful heart.
Numeracy helps the brain,
And doesn't drive you insane.

It can be boring,
When it is pouring.
It can be a game,
But sometimes can be lame.

Numeracy can be enjoyed,
Even if you are annoyed.
Numeracy can be exciting,
And is better than writing.

Numeracy is cool,
Better than playing pool.
You can be a fool,
If you're sitting on a stool.

Anthony Cropley (10)
Belah Primary School, Carlisle

Under The Sea

S ea horses are fun
E njoying the lovely sun
A t the bottom of the sea

H earing the sound of fish
O n the top of me
R eally enjoying my trip
S eeing dolphins flip
E nd of my trip, now to go home.

Jenna Horseman (10)
Belah Primary School, Carlisle

Monster!

Miss, there's a monster outside
And it looks really scary,
It's eating all the children Miss
And its belly's really hairy.

It's roaring like a lion Miss
Its horns are like spikes,
What are we going to do Miss?
Give it something it likes.

Run up a tree boy
Jump on its back
Try and kill it if you want
But don't come back.

I wonder what it's called Miss?
I wonder where it came from?
It's probably got a family you know
One dad, one mum, one sis.

I want to go home Miss
I'm not getting eaten
Please send me home Miss
And I won't be beaten!

Charlie Prudham (10)
Belah Primary School, Carlisle

The Diver

D eep in the sea
I n the dark, dark sea
V iolets, silver, golden, the colours I see in the blue
E ven in the darkest place is light with colours
R ushing in to see things before the cold sets in.

Stephen Byers (9)
Belah Primary School, Carlisle

Harry Kewell's Friends

Harry Kewell is so cool but sometimes he is a fool,
He jumps, he scores, he does it all
And he's great on the ball.
His other friend's called Paul, he's also great on the ball,
And his other mate Crouch is really, really tall.
His other friend is well hard his name is Steven Gerrard,
He also plays for Liverpool, just like Harry Kewell.
Harry Kewell plays for Liverpool,
And his brother's called Raul,
Raul is really good at sport and on his leg he has one big wart.
Harry is one of the best and he comes from the north-west,
He's the best in the city and he has two little kitties.

Scott Fawkes (10)
Belah Primary School, Carlisle

The Months

Winter is a good time of year with presents, joy and fun.
It comes only once a year with hardly any sun.

Summer comes once a year with plates of food and a giant pool.
They're times of year when we all want to be cool.

Autumn is the time of year when the leaves fall from the trees
And you don't see any bees.

The seasons are all different but all have something we like.
I like fishing in summer to catch a big pike.

Luke Sumpton (10)
Belah Primary School, Carlisle

Fire

His plug lit a spark
While he was sleeping,
Dreaming of going to the park,
And then he cried because of the noise.

The fire was noisily burning
He heard and went into his son's room
He couldn't stop his son from crying
He picked him up and wrapped a towel around him.

He threw the mattress out the window
He jumped out the window
He remembered about his wife and climbed back in
He couldn't find her, he thought she had gone.

He found her relief was in his eyes,
He picked her up and looked at her
As she was in his arms she died
He jumped back out the window
She was still in his arms.

He picked up his baby,
He couldn't stop either of them crying.

Lewis Fuller (10)
Belah Primary School, Carlisle

Hiding

Birds of prey at the start of May,
Looking in the hay,
Never stop to see them stare,
Because they're never there.

Swaying, swaying in the air,
You'll never see them there.
Looking for them, you will be
Until they swoop down now you'll see
The beauty which was hiding, hiding, hiding.

Simon Boothroyd (9)
Belah Primary School, Carlisle

Young Writers - A Pocketful Of Rhyme Northern Rhymes

Witchy Miss

Call the police now!
A witch is in my classroom
She's lighting all the candles,
Face red like a baboon.

She's conjuring an ancient spell,
I wonder what it makes,
Maybe lots of spiders,
Or bats or cats or snakes!

Oh no, I've found out what it does!
It's so horrendously sad,
I see a thousand sheets or so,
Of work (that makes her glad).

She's cackling in the winter's night,
Getting on her broom,
She laughs one final time and then
She flies out of the room!

I wonder, if you had seen this,
Would you have been as scared
Of teachers in the night as I?
(At least you'd be prepared!)

Let's hope that this time Hallowe'en
Will be as scary as this!
With red eyes glowing in the dark,
From my own Witchy Miss!

Johanna Armstrong (10)
Belah Primary School, Carlisle

Sea

S ilver sea shining
E verybody on the beach
A nd the people playing in the sea.

Adam Seymour (8)
Belah Primary School, Carlisle

The Shapes Are Dancing

Big and small and fat and thin
The shapes are dancing, make no sound
Large and fat and making a din
The shapes are dancing, make no sound
Bells and flutes and guitars and gongs
The shapes are dancing, make no sound
The king and queen where they belong
The shapes are dancing, make no sound
Up to bed all night long
The shapes were dancing, make no sound.

Camas Millar (9)
Belah Primary School, Carlisle

Shark

S wishing its tail
H aving to eat fish every day
A shark has razor-sharp teeth
R ushing and lurking through the deep blue sea
K illing all the fish.

Joe Ward (9)
Belah Primary School, Carlisle

Night!

Night is a vile, vicious creature,
He makes you feel sleepy and tired,
He has a crude purple face,
He has eyes of fire burning in a purply background,
His hair is as black as itself,
His clothes are made of dark leather,
He glides around the Earth slowly,
He speaks in a low, deep voice,
He lives in a dark cave with nothing but just darkness,
Night scares me.

David Robertson (10)
Markland Hill CP School, Bolton

Who Is She?

A dream-maker,
She has blazing blue eyes,
Her hair is thick, long and wavy,
Her face is pale but her eyes have a shadowy black outlining.

She wears a long silky dress,
With pink rosebud slippers,
Her slippers make a soft delicate sound on the floor,
She has purple gems in her hair.

She lives under a willow tree,
By a silvery moonlit stream,
She roams in the twilight,
The only sound is the flowing stream.

When she speaks it sounds as sweet as honey
Yet when day comes she runs home,
She hides in her palace of darkness,
Who is she?

Alex Fisher (10)
Markland Hill CP School, Bolton

Who Am I?

It is an evil, beastly time,
He makes me feel terrifyingly small,

His face looks like a ghostly mask,
His eyes are bright and sparkly like stars.

His mouth grins silently,
His hair unfolds as he glides through the sky,
His clothes are made of ebony leather,
He moves quickly across the land.

When he speaks the world takes a doze,
He lives in a dark enclosure.

He lives with his starry friends
He frightens me!

Daniel Cheetham-Taylor (10)
Markland Hill CP School, Bolton

The Dark Dream-Giver

A swift mover,
He relaxes me as he creeps across the floorboards,
Whispering a gentle tune,
His pale face haunts me as a glow shines off his snowy white skin,
His bright, glimmering eyes stare, paralysing me,
His mouth is frozen white like clear ice,
His navy blue face haunts me as a glow shines off his snowy
                                                    white skin,
His navy blue robes trail behind him as he strolls majestically,
He murmurs almost silently as his drained mouth shudders,
He lives in the shadowy mountain,
The dark clouds for company,
The only sound is the bold hoot of the owl,
Night is desolate and concealed beneath his ashen features.

Harriet Dagnall (10)
Markland Hill CP School, Bolton

Night!

Night is a thing that's nasty, also evil,
He makes me scared, all alone in my bed,
It makes me feel remote, lonely in my room
Then having nightmares,
His face is evil, red-eyed and bold,
He moves silently in the sky above the stars,
He lives in the big black galaxy,
He wears a black suit and is scared of the sun,
Then when the sun comes,
Night moves away,
To haunt another day.

James Boulton (10)
Markland Hill CP School, Bolton

A Hooded Figure

A hooded figure, with a face that cannot be seen by the human eye,
Piercing purple eyes hypnotise the mind and entrances it
Into terrible nightmares.
It is no friend.
It wears a black cloak, which trails along the dusty floor
And creeps from dawn to dusk in bare feet.
He speaks in a dark, low voice.
Lives in a small dark cave, also known as under your bed.
Hides in the day, comes out at dusk.
He is scared and unnerved by day.
Moves swiftly and glides off the ground like a black ghost.
Haunts you,
Ghastly revolting and nasty.

Eran Cotterill (10)
Markland Hill CP School, Bolton

Who Is He?

He is a cunning monster working all the time,
He makes me feel as small as an ant,
His face is a dark shadow hiding under his dark hood,
His eyes are purple, hypnotising your brain,
His mouth is a black hole,
His hair unfolds and spreads across the land,
His clothes are made of black snakeskin,
When he moves everyone trembles,
When he speaks the world sleeps,
He lives in a dark enclosure with the glistening stars and planets,
He frightens me.

Jaimie Booth (10)
Markland Hill CP School, Bolton

Night

He creeps unexpectedly
His only dread is light
'Go to sleep'
He calls from so far away.

I blunder in the land of dreams
Where everyone's happy
There's peace in the land
No war, no bullies,
No need for jail,
Just one happy world for me.

But he calls me to a dark mountain
Into his house
Where nightmares live
No one's happy
Everyone's angry
There are wars that never end.

This world is not for me
I run, I run, back home
Back to my warm, cosy room
Back to my cat at the end of my bed.

Eleanor Wilson (10)
Markland Hill CP School, Bolton

Night

Night is a time for demons
He helps robbers steal
Ghosts hide within him
He sleeps when dogs bark
His food is our fright
His eyes are black as coal
Mouth hollow and silent
Clothes made of fear
When he speaks, we sleep.

Harry Ward (10)
Markland Hill CP School, Bolton

That White Round Thing In The Dark Sky

A friendly and calm thing,
Which makes you all sleepy,
He is a comforting creature,
With kindness and care.
The night is a moonless hole,
In my dreams,
That's only one of the bad things.

Such a gentle and caring creature,
A kind face beaming down at you,
Only one moon for the Earth
A cheesy grin he has,
With two lovely grand eyes.

But it's 1-100 he creeps up on anyone,
Then flicks the switch that ends your day
Look out!
That switch is on you
Open to kill you
With no pain at all.

Ben Taylor (10)
Markland Hill CP School, Bolton

Who?

Creeping through the alleyways,
Wandering the Earth,
Darkening the cities,
A completely evil creature,
In dark, black robes.

Scaring many people,
Lounging on the world,
Darting all around you,
Barricading you in,
Afraid of daylight,
Who is he?

Bruce Pemberton-Billing (10)
Markland Hill CP School, Bolton

Night-Time

Night is a vile and vicious creature,
With dark inflamed eyes, it makes
Me feel so lonely, not safe.

Night is a creature that's black all over,
It speaks like a ghost and
Lives in the basement.

Night is coming to slaughter
You

Night is a soundless beast with
An evil voice and worrying
Vampire teeth.

Night is a gnome-sized mammal
That laughs horridly.

Night is coming to slaughter
You!

Charlie Howe (10)
Markland Hill CP School, Bolton

Who Is He?

An evil creature terrorising small children and forcing
Everyone to go to sleep.
Making me feel lonely and scared.
He covers his face with a big black hood.
Only his dark, red, evil eyes, piercing through.
He has no nose, no mouth, and no ears!
Wearing a long, black, creased gown with no holes,
Buttons or zips.
He creeps round supplying people with shivers and
Dreams.
He moves swiftly from dawn to dusk!
A ghoul that lives just above you.
But only comes to give you the creeps at night!
He has an enemy - *Day!*

Chloe Smith (10)
Markland Hill CP School, Bolton

The Night Demon!

'Bedtime,' called Mum,
Tired and weary I stooped upstairs,
And slowly, clambered in bed,
Drowsily I fell fast asleep . . .

But what I didn't know,
It was watching from above,
Eagle-like, it swooped down,
Wading swiftly towards my house.

Lingering above my parquet floor,
It cautiously approached my bed,
From under its shiny black robes,
A small, white, bony hand was unleashed . . .

As he let down his black hood,
Fiery red eyes pierced through me,
And he ran his bony fingers,
Along the middle of my short spine,
Turning dreams to nightmares,
Sending everyone straight to Hell!

Drew McGaughey & Rajan Bharaj (10)
Markland Hill CP School, Bolton

Hell!

Night is kind, comforting, safe,
Her sweet dream turns to a nightmare,
Boom! She turns back,
Her black hooded cloak covers her pale face,
Her eyes are fire
Lips burning-red
Hair black as night's sky,
Bang! It's *Hell!*

Hannah Aldcroft (10)
Markland Hill CP School, Bolton

Devastating Darkness

Darkness and shadows devouring light like a starved dog
Just waiting for you, creeping up on you.
The second you're in your bed you will be sound asleep
Night can do this!

Night
Can be a fog blocking off all light at night
And very soon, yes very soon, night will also
Be out of your sight!

Night brings coldness to all, sending a cold shiver down my spine
Night makes me lonely and scared,
But light conquers night and brings morning!

I am no longer scared
I am now ready for the day ahead!

Timothy Sinclair (11)
Markland Hill CP School, Bolton

Comets

Flying through space, pelting the stars to
Another galaxy,
Rapidly jumping from asteroid to asteroid,
Deciding which planet to bring vengeance on.
Twisting and turning,
Jumping up and down
Then finally falls to planet Earth!
Dodging every object at lightning speed building up more charge.
Frantically cutting a hole in the Earth
Making a new design.

Ben Laine (10)
Markland Hill CP School, Bolton

Night

Creeping through the dark alleyways
Scaring all the babies and little children
Running away when the sun comes out,
Only to come out again once it has gone,
You can never catch his cloak or him himself,
Furnishing people's dreams and no one can stop him
He's like a darkened ghost, forever wandering the darkened Earth,
Breaking into your subconscious and stealing valuables,
That's night.

Sola Nylander (10)
Markland Hill CP School, Bolton

The Haunted House

It howls in the bright silver moon of autumn,
Suddenly it opens its doors to the unfortunate petrified children
Outside in their terrifying costumes of Hallowe'en.
Its windows stare and spy at the surprised children in the
                                        bright moonlight,
Suddenly it jumps at them,
The wind whistles at them so hard that it makes the trees in the
Neighbourhood sprint out of their roots.

Ellie Schenk (9)
Markland Hill CP School, Bolton

CCTV Camera

The CCTV camera watches you furiously with its beady eyes,
It looks around everywhere looking for suspicious trouble,
It sees a car that's speeding
And as quick as a flash it blinks and takes a photo.
It looks at the photo carefully
Examining every inch
The camera spots a man in the car
And fines him £50.

Ellie McGivern (9)
Markland Hill CP School, Bolton

The Devil Of The Universe

A ghoul with a veil of hell covering her bloodshot eyes,
Clad in a flowing, black velvet gown with a black cotton cloak.
Lives in the depths of an abandoned, dark trench
In her poisoned skies,
Rides in a moonstone, diamond-encrusted chariot pulled by
enchanted stallions.
Feeds on bad dreams, the more she gets the more eclipses she
can create.
Flees from the sun in summer and in winter, takes over
the atmosphere.
A bewitched demon, she makes good dreams bad with a flash
of lightning.
Bullies the sun and is a deadly enemy to the sky,
Enchants the giants who roam the Earth.
Creates spooky, daunting thunder to create more and more
bad nightmares.

Night is the devil of the universe!

Java Entwistle (10)
Markland Hill CP School, Bolton

Fire

The windows were shaking, the barn was shuddering,
Fire was near running towards the horror-struck house,
The burning barn bellowed for freedom,
Bounding forward the fire clutched the trembling barn.

Bursting up into flames, the innocent barn cried, 'Stop, stop!'
The windows shattered,
'No one can stop me now!' chuckled the spiteful fire,
Smoke was filling the clear, blue air
It was too late, the barn had burned down.

Mary Axon-Smith (9)
Markland Hill CP School, Bolton

Night

He rides across the land on his horse of moonlight,
Bringing terror and despair as he goes.
A sly and spooky character, yet deep down misunderstood
He rides across the land on his horse of moonlight.

He rides across the land on his horse of moonlight,
The sun obliterated before him and his steed.
With slitted nose and veil of grief,
He rides across the land on his horse of moonlight.

He rides across the land on his horse of moonlight,
Piercing purple eyes and a dark robe of sorrow.
His gloves the souls of miserable people,
He rides across the land on his horse of moonlight.

He rides across the land on his horse of moonlight,
Shoes made by the living dead.
Over his heart a brisk plate of moonstone,
He rides across the land on his horse of moonlight.

He rides across the land on his horse of moonlight,
He moves on the sins of faraway prisoners,
But the sun has come up before him and his stallion,
He rides back to his mountain on his horse of moonlight.

Simon Hind (10)
Markland Hill CP School, Bolton

Night Is A Dangerous Person

A person of black magic and deep belief of witch's wizardry,
Living in the deepest crater on the dark side of the moon,
The skin, the lips with black tongue are pure venomous poison,
Her victims of nightmares are underground with a gravestone by
their head.

Dark secrets are still held at her feet,
Stay awake or suffer the fate.

Edward Hayes (10)
Markland Hill CP School, Bolton

Potion

The potion slurps and blows huge venomous bubbles,
It smells of tar and swallows masses of snowy white feathers,
The froth squeals as it gets hotter and hotter with fury,
The pot starts to scream and overflow onto the wooden floor.

The potion sinks into the floor underneath and down below,
The potion down below overflows with the almighty pressure
Of the potion up above in the room of the potion,
One sip of this potion . . . you will be . . . *dead!*

Anya Cotterill (9)
Markland Hill CP School, Bolton

The Rain

She sprints down to Earth, bouncing on the ground as she lands,
Shimmering as she walks down to Earth in a beautiful disco outfit,
She plays on an invisible trampoline bouncing as high as she can
$\qquad\qquad\qquad\qquad\qquad\qquad\qquad$ back up to the sky,
Singing loud jazz tunes at the top of her voice.

She feels happy and smiley, beaming at everyone she passes,
Crawling down roofs into gutters then sprinting quickly along them,
Jogging through the sky in her bed of clouds.

Lucy Entwistle (9)
Markland Hill CP School, Bolton

Crystal-White Fairies

The snow fairies dance and prance in the sky,
They sing with the wind in sweet voices
Whistling into passers-by ears.
It runs a white sparkling trail over every house and street.
It brings joy to children playing in the thick snow.
It twirls about in the air doing a show with all its friends.
It lands on the ground wriggling in a bed of white sheets.

Julia Sabery (9)
Markland Hill CP School, Bolton

A Special Bracelet

The sparkly, silver bracelet bathes in the warm summer sun,
Its eyes glitter in the moonlight as it turns dark navy,
It sleeps through the night,
Huddling under a silk scarf it finds.

Its thick, silver lining
Slowly glows into an ocean colour,
And happily waits for its owner.

When it is being worn,
It shimmers softly in the cool, calm wind,
Its pearly eyes sparkle,
As it is being shown to all the jealous customers.

Its rich, thin lining shows off to all its friends,
Dazzling their tiny eyes
The rich bracelet fades slowly into a cloud-white and
                                        turquoise mixture.

Leila Safi (9)
Markland Hill CP School, Bolton

The Garden

The garden huddles under a duvet of snow,
The trees whisper to each other as the wind glides by,
The holly leaves watch the balloon unexpectedly float past,
A thin lining of frost freezes on the helpless pond,
The snowflakes dance as they touch the soft ground.

Blazing summer comes by, leaves start to grow back,
The sun flicks a switch and summer pops up,
The sun walks up the stairs as it goes higher and higher in the
                                        boiling air,
As the day goes by the sun walks down the stairs,
And he makes the garden go black once again,
Winter approaches once more.

Robert Swinton (10)
Markland Hill CP School, Bolton

Water

Water glides through the ocean like a feather,
Water feels the roughness of all rocks,
The water in the ocean eats the bitter salt,
The water in a swimming pool drifts calmly.

Without water the ocean would be unsatisfied
Every grain of sand on the beach is the water's food,
When the tide comes in it is reaching for the food,
When the people come they are playing with the water's food.

The water runs to find India,
Jumping over boats and rocks,
All water lies down, the wind carries it along,
There is more water than land on the Earth.

Fergus Plant (9)
Markland Hill CP School, Bolton

Night

Night is dark, nasty and evil
He is very scary
With his red bulging eyes
He's up there somewhere making me lonely
He provides nightmares
He works in the dark like a burglar
With his coal-black hair
He has jet-black clothes
He moves at supersonic speed
Night lives in a cave with bats and rats
He will torture you.

Robert Winteringham (10)
Markland Hill CP School, Bolton

Jewellery

Dazzling necklace in the shop waiting to be bought,
Shouting out to the people going past, 'Buy me,'
Finally someone sees its sparkly jewels,
It gets picked up and put in a box,
Where it falls fast asleep in the box.

It suddenly gets taken out of the box and put in a jewellery box,
The necklace sneaks out of the box and runs downstairs,
It eats a mighty juicy hamburger,
It skips upstairs back into the box.

The necklace jumps to hug the owner around her neck,
She goes to the disco with her gorgeous necklace,
The necklace shone as it screams over the music,
'This is the best time of my life!'

Jennifer Walmsley (9)
Markland Hill CP School, Bolton

Fire

The flames flicker in every direction,
Sparking out of every hole,
Spitting on every object,
Flaming it up with fire.

Everything old, rusty and wooden will burn,
Trying to make its scampering run,
Bellowing for his revenge,
The fire takes them to their dreadful end.

Muhammad Karim (10)
Markland Hill CP School, Bolton

My Zip

My rusty, old zip cries with a whimper when I leave it hanging off the
edge of my jacket,
It hammers and clicks to its neighbour, so it can go zooming to
the top,
My mystified zip is never prepared to connect the hood!
It gets annoyed when the jacket sits down and my zip gets squashed.

It sometimes crawls up the jacket and unzips the hood,
The sneaky zip creeps and crawls up to the top of the slinky jacket,
and pretends to be king,
The weary, exhausted zip yawns because it's tired of all the
magical adventures,
It dreams that one day it can get out of the shop window.

Chloe Rothwell (9)
Markland Hill CP School, Bolton

Snow!

The snow swiftly jumps out the air to the floor below,
Snow hits the floor then it runs away with the wind,
The snow twists and turns in the air,
It quickly sprints onto people's skin,
The snow hits the ground then into the cold grass,
The snow plays races down to Earth,
When the snow is on the floor it talks to people when they walk past,
The snow cries frozen tears down to Earth,
The microscopic snow jumps to the gigantic Earth,
The snow sprints round the Earth.

Andrew Catterall (10)
Markland Hill CP School, Bolton

The CCTV

The CCTV watches you furiously
With its microscopic lens,
Zooms around and gazes at you one by one,
It screeches and hovers in its shimmering habitat,
No criminal will get away without being seen by the
Suspicious spying CCTV camera,
At night the secret staring CCTV doesn't sleep,
The only thing it eats is electricity and oil,
It may look like any old camera
But it has all the brand new technology,
The CCTV is suspicious, so watch out
It will see you.

Callum Rout (9)
Markland Hill CP School, Bolton

Star And Moon!

The moon glares down at the glowing Earth,
The stars sing in the shimmering dark,

The stars have a giggle as the aeroplanes go past,
As the moon is shining; it wears lots of pearls.

The moon hears a whisper in the air,
He hears all the babies crying down below.

The moon and the stars see everyone awaken,
They begin to go to sleep on the other side of the beautiful
                                        glowing universe!

Niamh Bolton (10)
Markland Hill CP School, Bolton

Fire!

Fire eats through the abandoned house
It spies through the dilapidated window
Fire yells so hysterically
That it diminishes the wood.

Fire smells like the sickening smell of bad breath
Fire feels like the red-hot feeling of when you're feeling sick
Fire sounds like the cracking of an ice lolly
Fire senses the smell of the abandoned house
Fire leaps across the world
It bellows across the tempting house.

Jack Dawson (9)
Markland Hill CP School, Bolton

Blizzards!

They throw themselves around and cover everything,
A blanket of white pleasure and gets scattered everywhere,
It fights off, it falls down to the ground softly,
Falling and turning, children covered in all of it,
Two clumps duel as they smack the floor,
Cover yourself up, freezing cold, get home quick,
White and deadly it runs and chases you,
Stare at it, it stares back!
Cold and trapped it hugs you to get warm,
Taps on the window, 'Let me in!' whistles the wind,
It is assertive against other things,
When clear you play out with it and be its friend.

Jack Hobson (9)
Markland Hill CP School, Bolton

After Evening

An old creature
Its evil glare stretching around the world
There is nothing he can't see
His dark purple cloak
Dotted with white blots
Night roams the Earth
Invisible to all
An indestructible foe
Its only fear . . .
Dawn.

Sam Mercer (10)
Markland Hill CP School, Bolton

Happiness

Happiness is purple and pink
It smells like roses in the field
It looks like a baby chick hatching out of an egg,
It feels like your heart has began a new life
It tastes as sweet as sugar
It sounds like a thousand smiles.

Naomi Craven (9)
Newton Bluecoat CE Primary School, Newton

Happiness

Happiness is a glittery pink,
It smells like treacle tart,
It looks like my mum's pink make-up bag,
It feels like bubblebath running through my fingers,
It tastes like squirty cream,
Happiness sounds like drum beats all around.

Lauren Sarjantson (10)
Newton Bluecoat CE Primary School, Newton

Anger

Anger is bright red
It smells like black smoke taking over the air
It looks like fierce faces all around you
It feels like hurting other people
It tastes like hot chillies
Anger sounds like lightning striking.

Samuel Hogarth (9)
Newton Bluecoat CE Primary School, Newton

Heartbreak

Heartbreak is black
It smells like fire burning wood
It looks like a funeral just waiting to happen
It feels like knives in my body
It tastes like blood from someone's body
Heartbreak sounds like your life shattering.

Russell Townsend (9)
Newton Bluecoat CE Primary School, Newton

Happiness

Happiness is a purply-pink.
It smells like a meadow of beautiful flowers.
It looks like a pair of polka-dot socks.
It feels like the fur of your favourite teddy.
It tastes as sweet as chocolate half-melted.
Happiness sounds like a baby bird's chirp.

Lauren Throup (10)
Newton Bluecoat CE Primary School, Newton

Love

Love is gentle red.
It smells like sweet lavender.
It looks like a baby bird waiting for its mother.
It feels like the softest, cuddliest, brown bear.
It tastes as sweet as raspberry cream.
Love sounds like a thousand love songs.

Tawana Gardner (9)
Newton Bluecoat CE Primary School, Newton

Jealousy

Jealousy is lime-green
It smells like petrol
It looks like they are showing it to you
It feels like a voice in your head telling you to buy it
It tastes like smoke burning in your mouth
Jealousy sounds like voices repeating in your head.

Joe Bench (10)
Newton Bluecoat CE Primary School, Newton

Love

Love is a soft red
It smells like a lavender perfume
It looks as sweet as a soft teddy
It tastes like hot chocolate
Love sounds like whistling birds.

Kirsten Milne (9)
Newton Bluecoat CE Primary School, Newton

Hate

Hate is dark grey
It smells like smoke
It looks like steamy hot fire
It feels like a punch in the stomach
It tastes as fiery as fireball jawbreakers
Hate sounds like an angry mob.

Rhys Llewellyn (9)
Newton Bluecoat CE Primary School, Newton

Happiness

Happiness is bright orange
It smells like sweet strawberries
It looks like bright flowers
It feels like soft silk
It tastes like melted chocolate
Happiness sounds like birds singing in a tree.

Georgia Jameson (10)
Newton Bluecoat CE Primary School, Newton

Love

Love is rosy red
It smells like pink blossom
It looks like little pink hearts
It feels like some toffee melting in your hand
It tastes like golden syrup
Love sounds like a thousand kisses.

Brittany Bee (9)
Newton Bluecoat CE Primary School, Newton

Happiness

Happiness is sky-blue
It smells like a white rose
It looks like a cute white lamb in the lush grass
It feels like a cosy warm bed
It tastes as sweet as strawberry sweets
Happiness sounds like birds singing in a tree.

James Hayhurst (10)
Newton Bluecoat CE Primary School, Newton

Anger

Anger is dark red
It feels like a tornado
It tastes as hard as toffees
It smells like thunder striking in the air
It sounds as hard as horns.

Abbie Ashworth (9)
Newton Bluecoat CE Primary School, Newton

Grief

G rief is like a piece of your life creeping away
R est in peace dear loved one
I n life you'll love someone just as much
E verlasting love feels shattered
F eeling grief drives you to do crazy things.

Joe Kearney (10)
Newton Bluecoat CE Primary School, Newton

Happiness

Happiness is bright blue
It smells like a rose
It looks like me hitting a six at cricket
It feels like me opening my cricket bat on Christmas Day
It tastes like eating chocolate
Happiness is like winning a bet with my dad.

Matthew Taaffe (10)
Newton Bluecoat CE Primary School, Newton

Hope

Hope is golden
It smells like a spoonful of sticky honey
It looks like the warm sun rising in the morning
It feels as good as a dive into the pool on a hot day
It tastes as delicious as runny golden syrup
Hope sounds like crowds of people cheering for you.

Catherine Davidson (10)
Newton Bluecoat CE Primary School, Newton

Love

Love is the colour of a rose
It smells as gorgeous as chocolate, it tastes like sweets on a hot
sticky day.
It looks like a million kisses in the morning.
It feels like my mum kissing me in the morning.

Alex Gamblin Thompson (9)
Newton Bluecoat CE Primary School, Newton

The Laughing Lizard

I was walking through the gloomy woods
When my eyes came to see
A lizard laughing at me
I asked him what he was laughing at
But then I heard a roar
So the lizard scampered
And I could see him no more.

Sophie Thomason (10)
Newton Bluecoat CE Primary School, Newton

Happiness

Happiness is sunshine-gold
It smells like the scent of a rose
It looks like stars relaxing in the night sky
It feels as soft as silk
It tastes as sweet as honey
Happiness sounds like the voices of angels.

Georgia Hallam (9)
Newton Bluecoat CE Primary School, Newton

Abstract Art!

A bstract art is full of dots,
B eautiful colours and pretty spots,
S ea-blue and crimson-red,
T o not do this art you will be dead,
R ed is really nice especially with brown,
A bstract art should be given a crown,
C ookie pictures are made,
T he art cupboard gets a raid.

A rt, art, wonderful art,
R eptiles are close to my heart,
T ogether all of them will look very, very smart.

Francesca Harrison (10)
Oldfield Brow Primary School, Altrincham

Ice Cream

Ice cream, ice cream,
We all scream for ice cream
Cooler than the Arctic ocean
Melting down in slow motion.
Ice cream, ice cream,
We all scream for ice cream.
It's one o'clock man, look at the time,
You'll have to be quick to get a Flake 99.
Ice cream, ice cream
We all scream for ice cream.
In the freezer waiting for sun,
Whenever we eat it we always have fun.
Ice cream, ice cream
We all scream for ice cream.
When I slept I dreamt I ate,
A really chewy monster flake.
When I wake I'm shocked to see,
I've lost my finger, number three.
Ice cream, ice cream,
I don't scream for ice cream!

Robert Shenkman (10)
Oldfield Brow Primary School, Altrincham

Fear

I'm grey like a dark, cold November night, as chills run down
my spine.
I'm the main culprit at Hallowe'en as the full moon falls down
I'm upon you, the one thing that people despise and hate at night
and day.
I'm the one thing that babies run from and get their parents for.
I'm the one thing that monsters and ghosts feed on at night.
Have you guessed?
I'm Fear.

Joshua Bower (10)
St Mary's RC Primary School, Ulverston

Boring Old School

School is so boring but let's make it fun!
The children take over, that's why we come!
We draw on the walls!
Scratch off the paint!
Scream at the teachers until they faint!
Plus, we make such a mess!
We are very naughty I must confess!
But hey, this is school,
The teachers are boring, that's why they drool!
But we make it fun, that's why children rule!

Peter O'Donovan (10)
St Mary's RC Primary School, Ulverston

The Werewolf

The werewolf lay low to the ground
Its wail echoed from the marsh
No one dared to move
Blood dripped from the beast's mouth every night
Till one night a blood-chilling cry shot out of the marsh
And the beast was dead.

Nathan Holmes (10)
St Mary's RC Primary School, Ulverston

Pets

Pets, pets what can I do?
They're doing their business all over my shoe.
I can't get it off
It must be stuck
Just my luck!

Scott Wilson (9)
St Mary's RC Primary School, Ulverston

Summer

Summer is brilliant,
Full of hot sun,
Wonderful holidays,
Time off school.
Summer is brilliant,
Lovely ice creams,
Many flavours,
Vanilla and mint.
Summer is brilliant,
Sunbathing on the beach,
Golden sand,
Wavy sea.
Summer is brilliant,
Making sandcastles,
With buckets and spades,
Shells and stones.
Summer is brilliant,
Looking in rock pools,
At crabs, jellyfish
And starfish too.
What a wonderful summer it is.

Abby Stack (11)
St Mary's RC Primary School, Ulverston

Butterflies

Tall, small,
Thin, fat,
Pink, black,
Up high in the sky,
Down low to the flow,
Wings out flat,
Wings tucked in,
Legs long,
Legs short.

Jodie Barber (10)
St Mary's RC Primary School, Ulverston

Are You OK Today?

Are you OK today?
Your throat looks rough
You need to cough so go to the doctor's OK?

Are you feeling better today?
You're burning up!
And you're in a knot.
Guess you're not better today.

You look better today
You've stopped burning up
You're not in a knot
You are better today . . .

Maddy Lackey (9)
St Mary's RC Primary School, Ulverston

Rugby

Mud is brown
Grass is green
You need a good team
To take out the Queen.

An oval ball
It's not football
The players are covered in mud.

But in the end
There's quite a bend
When you see the queue for showers.

Bradley Joy (10)
St Mary's RC Primary School, Ulverston

The Family Of Mice

There once was a lady called Laura
Who had a daughter called Aura.
She was nice enough
But kind of tough
Except when it came to the family of mice
Which lived in Aura's big bowl of rice.

When she turned on the light
She got such a fright
At the sight of those mice
Playing games of domino dice.
She would scream and shout,
Crying out, out, out,
But those mice, they were unmoved.

Laura was getting dreary,
And kind of weary,
At all this trauma
Being suffered by Aura.
She bought some freight
Which was an incredible weight.
She hoisted it up just high enough,
It was kind of tough.
The very next night she hid out of sight
And boy did she give those mice a fright!

Adam Bartlett (9)
St Mary's RC Primary School, Ulverston

Fear

Fear is black,
It sounds like thunder,
It tastes like getting stabbed.
It reminds me of a dark night,
And fear is red like fire-red.

Carl Postlethwaite (9)
St Mary's RC Primary School, Ulverston

Fear

Fear is a colour of flaming-red like a blazing fire
Spreading warmth throughout a dark and empty room.
Fear is the sound of a screeching scream in the middle of
a spooky forest.
Fear is a feeling of terror and loneliness.
Fear reminds you of somebody sitting in a corner of a dark and cold
Room, shivering every time the howls of thunder and the ripping of
lightning tear through the sky.

Callum Dixon (10)
St Mary's RC Primary School, Ulverston

Fear

The colour of fear is a dark red.
The sound of fear sounds like terrified screams.
The taste of fear tastes like horrible sick.
The feel of fear feels like hair of a tarantula.
Fear smells like sick.
Fear reminds me of hair of a tarantula.
What does fear remind you of?

David Wood (9)
St Mary's RC Primary School, Ulverston

Love

Love is pink like scented roses, with lovely yellow pollen
And bright green stalks.
It tastes like strawberry chocolate.
It feels like a really soft cushion.
It reminds us of married people.

Charlotte Penellum (10) & Alex Sansom (9)
St Mary's RC Primary School, Ulverston

School Drools

(Inspired by 'Please Mrs Butler' by Allan Ahlberg)

Mrs Ford, Mrs Ford
This girl Sheila Gool keeps burping in my face Miss,
What shall I do?

Mrs Fidler, Mrs Fidler
This boy Callum Drew keeps pushing me over,
What shall I do?

Mr Brown, Mr Brown
This boy Matthew keeps throwing paper aeroplanes,
What shall I do?

Kath, Kath
This teacher Miss Hardman keeps saying I'm a bully,
What shall I do?

Miss Leaver, Miss Leaver
This girl Georgia is leaving the school
She's my best friend Miss,
What shall I do?

Georgia Moore (9)
St Mary's RC Primary School, Ulverston

One December Night

The snowflakes are falling
Winter is nearby
Days are getting shorter
And the sun doesn't shine in the sky
Icicles are falling
And snow is here
And I get a slight feeling
That Father Christmas is near
The bells are ringing
It's a special day in December
Everybody's singing
This is a Christmas to remember.

Megan O'Donovan (9)
St Mary's RC Primary School, Ulverston

Fireworks

Remember remember the fifth of November
When it's Bonfire Night.
The burning flames dance and play games,
While cats and dogs fight.

The big starbursts are always first
Because they are just pleasant to see,
The amazing rockets people put in their pockets,
But that seems dangerous to me.

So that is the end and you cannot pretend,
That they will still hurt you.
Do be aware and please take care,
If you hold fireworks you can be burnt too.

Natalie Reynolds (10)
The Brow CP School, Runcorn

Easter Has Come

When I wake up and look on my bed,
I can see a pile of Easter eggs.

I go to my nan's to see what is there,
My nan says to look under the stairs.

I go to my friend's, she says, 'What have you got?'
I say to her, 'Nothing, I ate the lot!'

The next day has come, I feel much better,
My mum tells me to put on my warm, woolly sweater.

I go to my aunty's to see what she had,
She doesn't have anything, 'Phew!' I'm so glad.

Sophie McGuire (10)
The Brow CP School, Runcorn

Work

You know that thing your teacher gives you,
That thing you have to do,
Makes your brain begin to work,
Yes, it's that word again, *work!*

'Put your hand up,
Please don't shout,
Now go to your desks and get on with your work.'
Yes, it's that word again, *work!*

Turn the laptop on,
And type a poem,
Somebody puts their hand up, 'My PC won't work'
Yes, it's that word again, *work!*

Stop your brain from working,
Don't bother working,
Play games instead of typing,
Yes, that's the right type of *work!*

Mark Roberts (10)
The Brow CP School, Runcorn

Spring

Spring is here, it has begun,
Now is the time to have some fun!
Spring is the best season yet
New lambs are born, helped by the vet.

It feels like the flowers dance and sing,
The grass is growing nicely as I play on my swing.
At the end of the day, I'm so glad,
Spring is here and what fun I've had!

Susannah Pendlebury (10)
The Brow CP School, Runcorn

The Beach

I can hear the waves
And you can hear them too
Crashing on the seashore
Wondering what to do.

I can hear the dolphins
Squeaking like a mouse
I can see them jumping
Going to their house.

I can hear the seagulls
Squabbling over bread
They go round in circles
Around my head.

I can hear my mum and dad
Calling me for tea
So I pick up my bucket
And leave the sand and sea.

Sophie Sloan (10)
The Brow CP School, Runcorn

The Animal Park

I'd love to be a monkey to climb the trees,
Just like babies on their knees.

I'd love to be a tiger eating meat all joyful and happy,
They are not always a happy chappy.

I'd love to be an elephant all fat and round,
Always looking down on the ground.

Sam Hall (10)
The Brow CP School, Runcorn

Pets!

The things you cuddle for comfort, *pets,*
The things that eat your card sets,
Some we love and some we hate,
But most of the time they are our mates.

You can feel the warmth of their hair,
You can smell the grass on their coats,
You can hear them running with their feet racing,
You can touch their paw, feet, or hand with love.

You're sad when they have to go to the vet,
You wish you didn't have any other kind of *pet,*
You remember the first time you met,
But amidst all that you love them because they're your
    Pets!

Matthew O'Carroll (10)
The Brow CP School, Runcorn

The Dentist

It's that dreadful place that everyone hates,
The screaming and screeching goes through me like a knife.
Oh no! I need a filling,
I hope he doesn't start drilling.

Ha, ha! I'm late, hopefully he won't decide a dreadful fate
When I sit in that chair he starts laughing like an enormous
Grizzly bear!

Jamie Weeder (10)
The Brow CP School, Runcorn

What Is Yellow

What is yellow? The sun is yellow, like a shining light
What is red? A rose is red, in my back garden
What is blue? The sky is blue and it's very shiny
What is green? The grass is green, laying in my back field.

What is white? The cloud is white, floating in the sky
What is brown? The mud is brown, on a slippy field
What is orange? A car is orange, zooming past me
What is black? A pen is black, writing on a whiteboard.

What is silver? A fifty pence is silver, hiding in my pocket
What is gold? A ring is gold on my finger
What is black and white? A magpie is black and white
What is pink? A dress is pink and my mum is wearing it.

Thomas Grave (10)
The Brow CP School, Runcorn

Motorbikes

Start the engine, pull the throttle, click the clutch
And off you go.
Go up the jump, round the bend, pull a skid on the track.
Flicking mud in the air like mud hens flying everywhere.
There are all different kinds of them, some with two wheels,
Three wheels, and some with four wheels.

When you go up the jump ramp, do a backflip and land on
                                        the ground.
Rally along the track like a tall giraffe,
Round the corner, round the bend, pull a skid to the end of the track.

Ben Crank (11)
The Brow CP School, Runcorn

Confused

I kissed my bag
I packed my mum
I rubbed my dress
And put on my tum

I knocked for my car
I washed my nan
I looked for the loo
And he sat on the man

I made my TV
I watched my bed
I'm so confused since
I bumped my head.

Courtney Chamberlain (10)
The Brow CP School, Runcorn

The Bus

There it is again,
10 feet tall and ready to strike!
Zooming through a monstrous path,
The noise is booming through the street.

The smell is poisonous,
Don't breathe in!
Here it comes, racing towards you,
Please watch out, he's going to grab *you!*
His mind is set only on you!

So next time when you go on a bus,
Be careful now, watch out for us . . .

Nathan Merdassi (11)
The Brow CP School, Runcorn

The Zoo Animals

It's great to be a monkey,
Hanging from a tree,
But when you go to the park,
You really won't see me.

It's great to be a lion,
King of all the land
And I'm also,
King of the sand.

It's great to be an elephant,
All big, fat and round,
But when all the animals are looking up,
I'm looking down.

It's great to be a cheetah,
The fastest when I prowl,
But when you look up
All you'll hear is a growl.

Robyn Pattison (10)
The Brow CP School, Runcorn

Dragons

Big sharp teeth and a scaly tail
It gobbles up people, hear them wail!
Huge smelly feet, it's crushed a tree
Quick! Run! It almost squashed me!

Big wide mouth, as large as a tree,
'Argh!' Yikes! It's got me!
Down the neck and into the tum
Other people run, run, run!

Now down here, I'm going to be sick
I've got to get out of here very, very quick!
Yippee! I've found a way out!
That's all part of being a boy scout!

Joe McNally (10)
The Brow CP School, Runcorn

Dogs Are Cute

D ogs are cute, fluffy things
O h I love dogs so much
G ot to get one tomorrow or now, right now
S hannon loves dogs so much.

A re you getting one?
R ight, OK I will have that brown puppy,
E asy for me to look after one.

C ome and see my puppy,
U nder the fence, through the gate, we go for a walk.
T he little puppy is so still asleep, so cute,
E asy to choose a name for it, I think I will call
                                        it Pip.

Shannon Wright (10)
The Brow CP School, Runcorn

God's Garden

The trees are green,
Flowers colourful and refreshing
Rare animals you have never seen,
Bugs, creatures and birds singing.

Skies are blue, clouds silently moving,
Children are playing and full of laughter.
Sun is shining, the sea is glistening,
Orphans looking for homes to live happily ever after.

Talented people out there doing tricks,
Children in need, windows are open
Poor people make fires with sticks
This is the life in God's garden.

Alicia Knox (10)
The Brow CP School, Runcorn